Move It!

Bill Gaynor

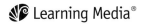
Learning Media®

Contents

Introduction

Every day, people push, pull, and lift things. Moving objects, both large and small, is a necessary part of life. Sometimes, this work is easy. Other times, it's more difficult, and we need to use a tool or machine to help us.

Most people imagine a machine to be something large and complicated with lots of moving parts. However, many of the machines that help us in our daily lives are actually very simple. A bottle opener and scissors are both machines called levers. Two other simple machines that we often use are pulleys and wheels. They help us move things from one place to another.

1. Gravity and Friction

Everyday chores are made more difficult by two forces: gravity and friction. Imagine you're stacking some boxes. As you work, you have to lift the boxes higher and higher and then push them into place.

Soon, you're tired, and your arms are aching. The work seems to be getting more and more difficult. This is because gravity and friction are working against you.

Gravity is the force that attracts objects to each other. Objects that have more **matter** have stronger gravity. A planet such as Earth has a lot of gravity, which pulls everything down toward the ground. The force of gravity keeps us on Earth's surface. Without it, we would float away!

The sun, which is much larger than Earth, has a powerful force of gravity. This attracts all of the planets in our **solar system** and keeps them in their **orbits**.

Life without Gravity

Imagine living on a planet that has no gravity. Many jobs, such as stacking boxes, would be a piece of cake. In fact, you could move anything you wanted, no matter how heavy it was, because nothing would have weight. Even your body would weigh nothing. So, you'd waste less energy on work, and you'd also save energy because your muscles wouldn't need to support your body's weight. Life in zero gravity would be no effort at all.

Unfortunately, there's a downside to life without gravity – just ask any astronaut. Anything not tied down floats away, making it difficult to keep track of your possessions. Drinking water from a glass is also a problem because even the water floats away.

Friction is the force that causes objects to **resist** being moved across each other. For example, when stacking those boxes, you have to push hard to get them in the right position. If friction didn't exist, a small shove would be enough to move each box into place.

Moving parts

Oil

In a machine with moving parts, such as a bicycle, there's a lot of friction. Oil and grease are used to help these parts slide over each other more easily.

Rough Work

If you pull something over a smooth surface, the object should move easily. However, if you move the same thing over a rough surface, you'll notice that you have to pull harder. This is because there is more friction with a rough surface.

You can see this for yourself with a block of wood. Drag the wood over a smooth surface such as a table, using a rubber band. You'll notice that the rubber band stretches a little before the block begins to move.

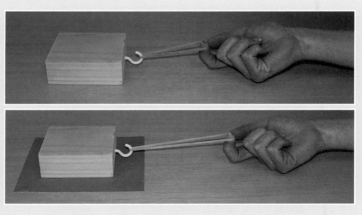

Now try dragging the wood over a rough surface, such as a piece of sandpaper. The rubber band will stretch a lot more because you're pulling much harder – and you have to pull harder because there's more friction.

If there were no such thing as friction, it would be easier to move things around, but the world might be a trickier place to live in. For example, riding a bike would be more dangerous because there would be nothing keeping your tires gripped to the ground. Riding on a road with no friction would be as slippery as riding on ice.

So it's lucky that friction and gravity do exist. Better still, we have simple machines such as wheels, levers, and pulleys to help us overcome these forces.

2. Wheels

The wheel was one of the most important early inventions. Before wheels, people had to carry things on their backs, no matter how heavy the load. Because the first people were hunters and gatherers, they were always on the move in search of food. Having no wheels to help transport their possessions must have made life especially difficult for them.

In time, prehistoric people learned to build sleds. They made these from poles and logs and used them to drag loads over long distances. Later, they added runners to the sleds, helping them to slide more easily across the ground.

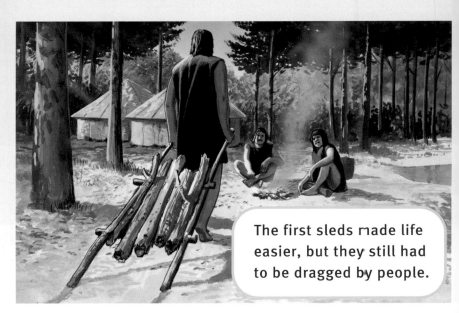

The first sleds made life easier, but they still had to be dragged by people.

Around 5000 BC, people began using animals like donkeys and oxen to carry their loads. When wheels were invented, they could hitch these animals to carts and wagons. This meant that they could transport heavy loads, such as grain and wood, over longer distances.

In some parts of the world, carts and oxen are still used to transport goods and people.

The First Wheels

Long ago, people used logs as rollers to move heavy loads. It's thought that the first wheel was based on this idea. The first wheel to have an **axle** was invented in **Mesopotamia** around five thousand years ago. Because they were made from solid wood, these early wheels were very heavy and tricky to use.

Around 2000 BC, the Egyptians began using wheels that had **spokes**. Wheels with spokes were much lighter than wheels made from solid wood, and they made carts and **chariots** a lot easier to steer.

Later, people added iron rings to wheels, which protected the wood and helped the wheels to last longer. However, these iron rings didn't prevent the problem of a bumpy ride. People had to wait until the nineteenth century, when rubber tires were invented, before they could enjoy a bump-free ride.

Once people began to live in villages and towns, they wanted more solid buildings. In many places, stone became a popular building material. However, as you can imagine, moving blocks of stone was hard work. Luckily, in many parts of the world, people had wheels, so they could use carts to make construction work faster and safer. Workers also used less effort because wheels helped them overcome the problem of friction.

Point of friction

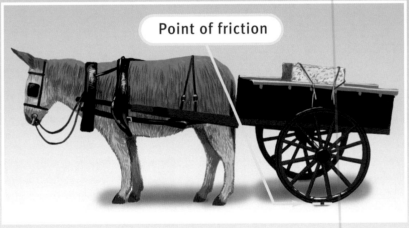

Point of friction

Using a cart instead of a sled made the work of moving a heavy load much easier. This is because only a small part of the cart's wheels rubs against the ground at any one time, which reduces the amount of friction.

Today, we use so many wheeled machines to move loads it's hard to imagine life without them. A delivery person uses dolly wheels to move packages or boxes, and a gardener or construction worker moves soil or building materials with a wheelbarrow. Trucks, buses, cars, and bicycles also make the work of getting from one place to another much easier, especially if you're moving a load.

3. Levers

A lever is a simple machine that helps us with everyday tasks. If you can't get the lid off a can, you might use a spoon as a lever. Scissors, a **crowbar**, and a wheelbarrow are also common levers, which help us do work with less effort.

A lever is a bar that moves on a point called a fulcrum. The bar and fulcrum work together to move a weight, called the load. The load is usually at one end of the bar. The pushing movement that's needed to lift the load is called the effort.

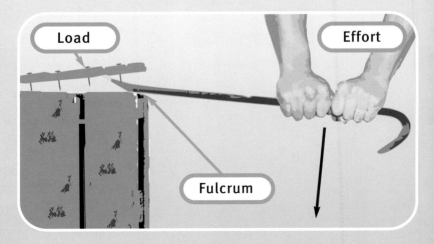

Load

Effort

Fulcrum

The Greek **mathematician** and inventor Archimedes was one of the first people to discover how levers work. He thought that it was possible to move anything if you had a lever that was long enough. He even claimed that if he had a big enough lever and fulcrum, he could move the world.

Give me a lever long enough and a place to stand on, and I will move the earth.

– Archimedes, 230 BC

There are two main types of lever: first-class levers and second-class levers. A first-class lever has the fulcrum in the center. A person pushes down on one end of the bar, which lifts the load at the other end. Even though it's used for playing, a seesaw is an example of a first-class lever. The board that each child sits on is the bar, the fulcrum is the point in the middle that the seesaw balances on, and each child takes a turn at being the load.

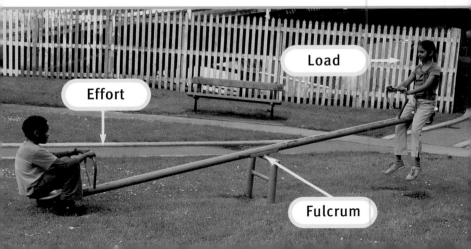

Effort

Load

Fulcrum

Using a long lever also helps to make the work easier. Imagine trying to move a heavy rock with a short stick. It would be difficult or even impossible to do. However, if you used a longer stick, the rock would move more easily.

Levers often work in pairs, such as in scissors, nutcrackers, wire cutters, and pliers. Pairs of levers are useful for gripping, cutting, or squeezing things.

Scissors

Nutcracker

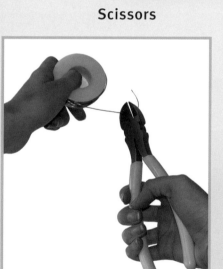

Wire cutters

Pipe pliers

Levers Working Together

In a pair of pliers or wire cutters, the fulcrum is the point where the two halves of the tool are joined. A person provides the effort by squeezing the jaws of the pliers or wire cutters shut.

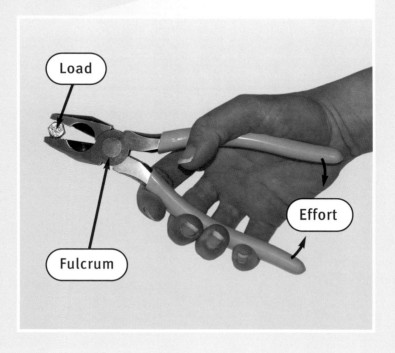

Load

Fulcrum

Effort

In a second-class lever, the fulcrum is at the end of the bar and the load is in the middle. A wheelbarrow is an example of a second-class lever. The axle through the middle of the wheel is the fulcrum, the load is the material being carried in the wheelbarrow's tray, and the effort is supplied by the person lifting the wheelbarrow.

Load

Fulcrum

Effort

Body Levers

Even your body has its own pairs of levers. When you chew, your jaw muscles pull the two halves of your jaw together – just like a nutcracker! Your jaw is a simple lever that helps with the important work of eating!

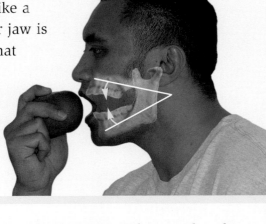

When you pick something up with your thumb and finger, your bones (with the help of your muscles) act as levers. You use these same bones and muscles to cut something using a pair of scissors.

23

4. Pulleys

If you've ever watched a crane working on a construction site, you'll know how useful a pulley can be. A crane lifts heavy objects using a powerful motor and a system of pulleys.

The most basic kind of pulley has a wheel with a rope wrapped around it. This rope is attached to the load that's going to be lifted. Simple pulleys were first used centuries ago when workers needed help lifting things such as blocks of stone.

Long ago, pulleys were used to help build churches and castles, which were usually made from stone.

Whether a worker carries a load to the top of a building or hauls on a pulley's rope, they're still using the same amount of energy. However, a pulley is still useful because it's usually a much safer way of moving a load than carrying it. This is because the person has more control, especially if the ground is slippery or uneven.

In the past, it was safer to lift blocks of stone with a pulley than to carry them up a ladder or a flight of stairs.

A two-wheeled pulley makes the work of lifting something even easier.

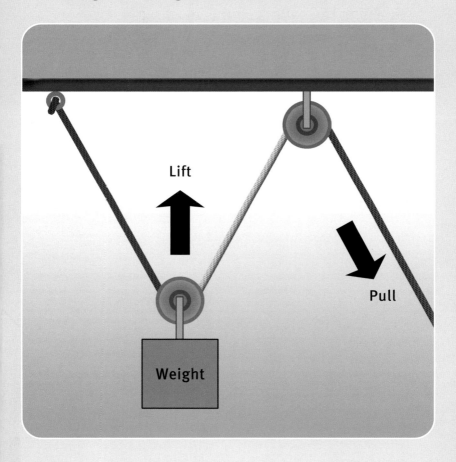

This load is being lifted by two sections of rope (one red and one yellow). Each section is sharing the weight of the object.

Using Pulleys

See for yourself how a two-wheeled pulley makes lifting things easier.

You will need:
- two pulley wheels
- some string
- a rubber band
- a small weight.

1. First, try using just one pulley wheel.

   Thread the string over the pulley and tie the rubber band to the end. Lift the weight and see how far the rubber band stretches.

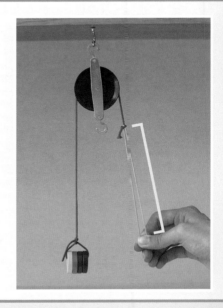

2. Now try using two pulley wheels.

Lift the weight again. The rubber band doesn't stretch as far. This is because it takes less effort to lift a weight using a two-wheeled pulley.

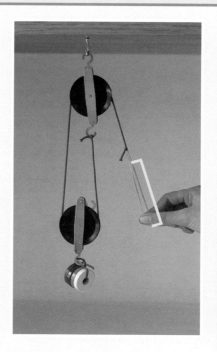

The more wheels you add to a pulley, the easier it will be to lift the weight. This is because the work is being shared between the different sections. The pulleys on cranes often use several wheels, which means that less effort is required to lift a load. More importantly, it means that the crane uses less fuel.

Conclusion

Since ancient times, people have looked for ways to make their work easier. The invention of wheels, levers, and pulleys made many chores much easier. These simple machines were first used thousands of years ago, and they still a low us to push, pull, and lift almost anything we want.

The transporter used to move a spaceshuttle is the largest vehicle ever made.

Glossary

(These words are printed in bold type
the first time they appear in the book.)

axle: the rod that goes through the center of
a wheel

chariot: a horse-drawn cart that was used by
rulers and warriors

crowbar: a steel bar that's used as a lever

mathematician: an expert in math

matter: the material that an object is made up of

Mesopotamia: an area that is now part of Iraq

orbit: the path followed by a planet as it circles
the sun

resist: to fight against something

solar system: the sun and its planets

spoke: the thin metal bars that go from the
center of a wheel to its edge

INDEX